Mindful living
JOURNAL

JOURNALLING PRACTICES FOR
A SACRED AND HAPPY LIFE

KATIE ROSE

ROCKPOOL

introduction

Welcome to the *Mindful Living Journal*. Journalling has been a huge part of my life ever since I can remember. As a young girl I went to church in the small English village I grew up in and was given a copy of the Bible; the first journal I remember keeping was a notebook in which I wrote about my thoughts and ideas from reading that Bible. I wasn't in a formal process of study or teaching in this endeavour and as a result I'm sure my notes were a little random and haphazard, but it was in those notes I found a love for the written word and the ordering of my thoughts that went with it. To this day if I am upset, overwhelmed or confused I'll reach for a notebook and pen and start processing through writing.

A few years ago I got divorced and as a result had a lot of life tidying to do both on the energetic plane and in the practical realm. In the process of moving to a new house I came across boxes of notebooks I'd kept in storage, some of which dated back to my teenage years. I spent an emotional afternoon flicking through many of them (so many truly cringe-worthy moments there!), and what struck me the most was how much of a friend the written word has been to me. In these days of text and email and meme there is something so precious and irreplaceable about a long-form written note, letter or reflection. Writing in my journals and notebooks is a habit I don't see myself giving up any time soon, and it's my heartfelt wish that the guidance in these pages will inspire your journalling practice to become lifelong if you don't have one already. Here are some ideas and suggestions about journalling to contemplate before we begin:

- » Handwriting is best; typing just isn't the same. Research indicates our brains work differently when we actually write words down rather than typing them (we remember differently too, which can be helpful if you're studying for an exam or setting an intention you really don't want to forget).
- » Journalling can be a practice that evokes mindfulness, the experience of which happens whenever we drop into being fully available for the present moment;

we're not languishing somewhere in a past dream or projecting forward into a fantasy future. In true mindfulness we are engaged in the here and now. Often when journalling we will reflect on the past or plan for the future, but the magic of journalling really unfolds when we anchor into the present moment. Journalling on the subject of gratitude can help us to become present, which is why in this *Mindful Living Journal* we start with a gratitude practice to anchor into both remembering the blessings in life already and becoming truly present in this precious moment.

» Your writing can be as structured or as free form as you like. You don't have to write in full sentences or tidy bullet point lists, as you are writing for yourself, not public presentation. In the next few pages I'll suggest and give an example of a 'mind map' as one alternative way of journalling, but really the sky is the limit. Go with your flow, and if you feel called to draw and illustrate your journal all the better.

» There are no rules and you don't have to show anyone. A good friend and spiritual sister recently gave me the advice of writing down all my grief, sadness and confusion. It was a great suggestion, but there was a part of me that kept self-editing because somehow writing down words that reflected how I was feeling seemed to set them in stone. I worried that someone might see them or I might come back to them at a later date and be filled with remorse and regret. The antidote to this was suggested by my friend: burn the words after you've written them. That's right: get it all out and then set it on fire! I can't tell you how much relief this burning process has given me. Burning words you want to eliminate from your life is particularly powerful during a full moon, but you can create your own letting go ritual and you will find it incredibly cathartic.

» Journalling can really help you with achieving goals. If you can't imagine a future possibility or put words to it then it will be much harder to manifest. You can start small and get bigger; for instance, you might start with tweaking your morning routine to include more connection to your spiritual self and less rushing. Journal a small list of changes such as getting up 10 minutes earlier to meditate, making time for breakfast or pausing to set an intention. This approach can then be amplified to much bigger goals such as attracting an intimate partner into your life who is aligned with your values and dreams or taking your career to the next level.

» Strengthen self-discipline through your journalling. Sometimes it's wonderful to daydream and spend time journalling a fantasy (hello, holiday home by the beach!), but journalling can also help you to achieve those goals if you are diligent. For example, with a big goal it might be helpful to break it down into individual pieces. Journalling for goal setting can also help you become clear about your intentions in certain areas of your life. Perhaps your home is getting messy and disorganised and you need to do a big spring clean, so how can you break this overwhelming task into manageable pieces? Or maybe you want to start a new fitness regime, and journalling about it can make your next actionable steps really clear.

» Journalling is a healing practice. We all experience times of grief and sadness in life and writing about them can help you process what you're going through. When you are faced with a break-up, death or another loss, journalling can be a powerful way to process the emotions that come up. Likewise, big life transitions such as moving house or changing your job can be supported by a journalling practice.

Before we dive into the specific areas of journalling as guided by the *Mindful Living Journal*, let's set a solid foundation by reflecting on where you're starting. Take the next few pages of this introduction as an opportunity to make an appraisal of where your life is at right now. As you go through this process there will be areas that feel like strengths, areas in which you are shining and radiant. There will be other areas where you feel disappointed with yourself and 'less than'. Stay open to both, and to all the shades of grey in between. There can be no light without darkness, and we can't all be good at everything!

As I've grown in spiritual maturity, one of the things I've learned is that it's refreshing and even relaxing to acknowledge the things I'm not good at. I'm never going to be patient enough to knit myself a jumper, and I'm probably not going to master playing the piano in this lifetime. Knowing these things about myself is okay, as it means I can stop striving for everything and can get really focused on where I want to pour my energy. Instead of feeling bad that I'm not particularly musically talented, I can enjoy singing at the weekly kirtan (chanting) events I attend. Instead of wishing I could knit (or sew!), I can enjoy shopping in vintage stores and appreciate the craftsmanship that went into clothing made in another era when skill and time were poured into slow fashion as an art form. This approach takes all pressure off; it's such a relief! I don't have to make or own or be it all, and can appreciate other people's talents as being different to my own and show up in the world expressing my own talents as fully and beautifully as possible.

As you step into the world of journalling, embrace not only the light in yourself that you celebrate but also the challenges and darker corners, and do so without judgement or low self-esteem but rather as a celebration of who you are and what you have to offer the world. Remember: no one need ever see your journal, as it is your private space where you can express your innermost journey. With this in mind, let's take stock and begin the journalling journey together.

love, katie

WWW.BHAKTIROSE.COM.AU

how to use the journal

The journal loosely follows the journey from the foundations of who we are to spiritual aspirations of our highest selves, so there is a sequential element to it and you can work through from beginning to end if you choose. That said, you might also wish to dip in and out of particular areas that call to you or seem pertinent at the time. Use your intuition and journal in the way that best supports your growth and joy.

introduction to journalling

The following introductory pages set the foundation for your journalling practice and for you to review where you're at in your life right now. Feel free to write in list format, draw a mind map or even create a visual representation of your answers to these prompts. It's your own practice of journalling, so make it work for you. I've created a gratitude mind map based on my own life to give you some creative stimulation.

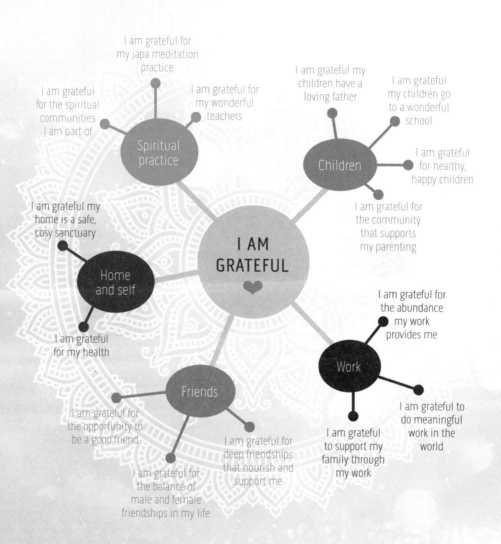

What are you grateful for in your life right now?

When answering the following question be as specific as possible, for example, in my own life I am grateful for my mother and I speaking more frequently on the phone in the last few weeks.

What are you grateful for in the realm of family right now?

_____

_____

_____

_____

_____

_____

_____

_____

_____

_____

_____

_____

_____

_____

_____

_____

_____

_____

_____

_____

_____

_____

_____

_____

WHAT ARE YOU GRATEFUL FOR IN THE REALM OF WORK RIGHT NOW?

Pull success into your energy field, your aura, and fully participate in everything that is required to make your success a reality. **How can you be the artist of your own success, however you may define it?**

_____

_____

_____

_____

_____

_____

_____

_____

_____

_____

_____

_____

_____

_____

_____

_____

_____

_____

_____

_____

_____

_____

_____

_____

What are you grateful for in the realm of your spiritual life and practices right now?

WHAT ARE YOU GRATEFUL FOR IN THE REALM OF FRIENDSHIPS RIGHT NOW?

List your close friends and write down what you treasure in each of them.

WHAT ARE YOU GRATEFUL FOR IN THE REALM OF YOUR HOME RIGHT NOW?

Which room in your home is your favourite and why?

What do you treasure about your home?

Reflect on your life as being abundantly full of love and support. It's easy to see what is not there, and the material society we live in depends on us striving for more, more, more and in turn feeling inadequate. Instead, how can you see what is already present? Shift focus to what is truly of value in your life such as relationships and not material things. **What community support is flourishing in your life right now?**

How could you show up in loving service and make a deeper contribution to the communities you live in?

_____

_____

_____

_____

_____

_____

_____

_____

_____

_____

_____

In being of service to others, support will be there for you when you most need it (and often in the most unexpected ways). **How can you serve the communities in your life more deeply?**

_____

_____

_____

_____

_____

_____

_____

_____

_____

_____

STEADY
FOUNDATIONS

living a life of compassion and kindness is the highest spiritual ideal

In the ancient Indian language of Sanskrit (the yogi's language) this is called *ahimsa*. Although we can apply ahimsa to ourselves the usual application is towards others; the yogi prioritises offering loving kindness to others. **How can you amplify ahimsa in your life to become a more compassionate person?**

_____

_____

_____

_____

_____

_____

_____

_____

_____

_____

_____

Think about areas such as your behaviour and work and the food you eat.

_____

_____

_____

_____

_____

_____

_____

_____

_____

_____

BHAKTI IS ANOTHER SANSKRIT WORD, MEANING 'LOVING DEVOTION'

The things in your life that you devote yourself to either expand your energy or deplete it. To practise bhakti is to dedicate your life to the highest good. **How can you become more devoted to the values of beauty, love, kindness and joy in your life?**

_____

_____

_____

_____

_____

_____

_____

_____

_____

_____

_____

_____

_____

_____

_____

_____

_____

_____

_____

_____

_____

_____

_____

_____

_____

_____

Non-violence is the foundation of all yoga practice as well as Buddhism; a positive way of expressing this is to live in compassion and kindness. An easy way to start applying ahimsa into your life is to eat less animal products, for which there will also be benefits to your health and the environment. My teacher Sharon Gannon, co-founder of the Jivamukti Yoga method, always encourages us to be joyful vegans. There is no need for anger, judgement or defensiveness: we can choose to be kind and happy! **How can your diet be more aligned with your values?**

the things you do every day make up your life

What things do you do every day that light you up?

_____

_____

_____

_____

_____

_____

_____

_____

_____

_____

_____

_____

_____

_____

What is depleting and draining in your life?

_____

_____

_____

_____

_____

_____

_____

_____

_____

_____

_____

_____

_____

_____

Sadhana means 'conscious spiritual practice' and is usually made up of the small rituals and routines that support your daily life. Some habits hold us back from progress (for example, smoking or reaching for junk food when you feel stressed), while others fortify our energy (for example, meditation or physical exercise). **Where can you cultivate more positive habits in your routines and rituals?**

_____

_____

_____

_____

_____

_____

_____

_____

_____

_____

_____

_____

_____

_____

_____

_____

_____

_____

_____

_____

_____

_____

_____

_____

SWEET SPEECH

Gossip drains both the person speaking and the person listening. **Who do you know that inspires and uplifts you when you talk to other people? What kinds of things do they say?**

_____

_____

_____

_____

_____

_____

_____

_____

_____

_____

_____

_____

_____

_____

_____

_____

_____

_____

_____

_____

_____

_____

_____

_____

If you are unsure whether or not you are gossiping, follow this simple rule of thumb: ask yourself 'Is what I'm about to say bringing the people I'm speaking about closer together or dividing them?' Usually when we are gossiping it creates division. **Where are the places in your life that pull you into gossip? How can this habit be transformed?**

_____

_____

_____

_____

_____

_____

_____

_____

_____

_____

_____

_____

_____

_____

_____

_____

_____

_____

_____

_____

_____

_____

_____

_____

_____

Speak for the voiceless, as it is an act of spiritual activism to speak up for those who are marginalised or do not have a voice. **Where in your life can you speak up on behalf of another who is not or cannot speak for themselves?**

_____

_____

_____

_____

_____

_____

_____

_____

_____

_____

_____

_____

_____

_____

_____

_____

_____

_____

_____

_____

_____

_____

_____

_____

Satsang is a Sanskrit word that means 'keeping the company of the truth' or, in other words, hanging out with people who are uplifting and inspiring. **Who inspires you and leaves you feeling that life is full of possibilities? How can you spend more time with these people?**

SACRED SILENCE: THERE IS ENORMOUS GRACE IN KEEPING QUIET SOMETIMES

Think back to the last time you said something you regretted. **What was the sequence of events that led to this outburst? How could it be avoided next time?**

_____

_____

_____

_____

_____

_____

_____

_____

_____

_____

_____

_____

_____

_____

_____

_____

_____

_____

_____

_____

It's easy to get swept up in the small details of life and forget our big dreams and goals. **What are the bigger picture aspirations you want to keep close to your mind and heart?**

More than ever we live in a world of distraction and instant gratification, yet we know that most things worth achieving take diligence and discipline. **What could you cut out of your life in order to be more focused, such as TV, social media, procrastination?**

_____

_____

_____

_____

_____

_____

_____

_____

_____

_____

_____

_____

_____

_____

_____

_____

_____

_____

_____

_____

_____

_____

_____

_____

WHAT COULD YOU ADD INTO YOUR LIFE TO HELP YOU WITH PRODUCTIVITY?

Some of the most successful people in the world start their day with attending to very important tasks before they get drawn into answering emails or other distractions. **What are the things you really want to prioritise in your day and in your life at this time?**

_____

_____

_____

_____

_____

_____

_____

_____

_____

_____

_____

_____

_____

_____

_____

_____

_____

_____

_____

_____

_____

_____

If you often snack on junk food when energy is low in the late afternoon, could you prepare a healthy green smoothie for that time instead? Think creatively. **What daily habits impact negatively on your health? What could you do to change them?**

_____

_____

_____

_____

_____

_____

_____

_____

_____

_____

_____

_____

_____

_____

_____

_____

_____

_____

_____

_____

_____

_____

_____

_____

_____

_____

_____

_____

Energy cleanse yourself and your loved ones: whenever you return home from a busy day, how can you get grounded and leave the problems of the world at the door so they don't have an impact on your most important relationships? Perhaps you could burn some incense or sage to clear and clean the energetic space around you. **What else could you do?**

_____

_____

_____

_____

_____

_____

_____

_____

_____

_____

_____

_____

_____

_____

_____

_____

_____

_____

_____

_____

_____

_____

_____

_____

Dream up a vision of an altar or sacred space in your home that would make your heart sing. **What would be on it? How would it be adorned?** Mine is abundant with roses!

_____

_____

_____

_____

_____

_____

_____

_____

_____

_____

_____

_____

_____

_____

_____

_____

_____

_____

_____

_____

_____

_____

_____

_____

_____

_____

Whimsical beauty: whether through formal arts such as photography, drawing or creating, or through less formal ways such as how you dress or decorate your home, most of us have some creative outlet that enhances our lives. Part of amplifying mindfulness in our lives can include paying more attention to these creative opportunities. Presenting food beautifully before serving it, lighting a candle or even cleaning your home are all ways to reconnect to the inner creative spirit when you do them with the right vibe and intention. **How do you express beauty and creativity in your daily life?**

_____

_____

_____

_____

_____

_____

_____

_____

_____

_____

_____

_____

_____

_____

_____

_____

_____

_____

_____

_____

_____

_____

_____

_____

space cleaning

As well as clearing your own energy or aura you can practise energetic cleansing of your home and work spaces. Whether you burn sage to cleanse with smoke or strategically place crystals around your space to lift the level of vibrations, taking care of the energy, the vibes, in your surroundings will aid you in clarity, concentration and creativity. It's said that your external environment is a reflection of your internal mental landscape. Next time you feel a little out of sorts, try cleansing your space and see if it helps you to come back into alignment. **How can you lift the vibration level in your home?**

_____

_____

_____

_____

_____

_____

_____

_____

_____

_____

_____

_____

_____

_____

_____

_____

_____

_____

_____

_____

DECLUTTER AND CLEAR!

Which areas in your home are energetic black holes?

_____

_____

_____

_____

_____

_____

_____

_____

_____

_____

_____

_____

_____

_____

What can you declutter or move around to create a more welcoming living space?

_____

_____

_____

_____

_____

_____

_____

_____

_____

_____

_____

_____

Many of the flowers you buy in a florist or supermarket have had a huge environmental footprint because of spraying and transporting, and that's even before they've been wrapped in plastic and adorned with pretty ribbons. A hand-picked bunch of local foliage or a plant are much more environmentally friendly choices and usually cost less as well. **How do you beautify your home?**

_____

_____

_____

_____

_____

_____

_____

_____

_____

_____

_____

_____

_____

_____

_____

_____

_____

_____

_____

_____

_____

_____

_____

SACRED
OUTLOOK

Think happy, be happy; or as one of my first yoga teachers, Simon Low, says: 'Where the mind goes, energy flows.' Pay attention to what you put into your mind in terms of the media you consume; violent and scary movies, for example, leave an imprint in your psyche. **What type of media uplift and inspire you? What leaves you feeling drained?**

YOUR MIND IS VERY IMPACTED BY THE INPUT COMING INTO YOUR AWARENESS VIA THE SENSE GATES

Aromatherapy works with your sense of smell. Clary sage essential oil is one of my favourite remedies to ease symptoms during my menstrual cycle; I also love rose essential oil to uplift my mood at any time of the month! **What are your favourite essential oils and when do you like to use them?**

Surrounding your home with beautiful fragrances or taking a walk outside after a rain shower are two ways to engage your sense of smell to uplift and revitalise. Perhaps you love the smell of home-baked treats in the oven or freshly ground coffee. **How can you bring more aromatherapy into your life by celebrating the fragrances you surround yourself with?**

nurturing touch: where in your life do you give and receive nurturing touch?

Could you make time for a massage or create a sacred intimate space with your lover to enjoy sensual touch?

Who would benefit from a hug today?

Making time for each other: one of the biggest challenges of the age we live in is that we are more connected than ever but less present for each other. **How can you improve the quality of the time you spend with loved ones?**

phoenix rising!

I love the myth of the phoenix (and named one of my sons after it): we can rise up out of the ashes of our own trauma, fear and struggles. The practices of yoga and meditation give us the tools to become the best version of ourselves if we apply them diligently. **What difficult situations in your life have you risen out of and learned from?**

Mine the gold: sometimes we have to do the heavy lifting to shift a lot of dead weight before we get to the gold. **Where in your life do you need to clear the way to find the gold?**

_____

_____

_____

_____

_____

_____

_____

_____

_____

_____

_____

_____

_____

_____

_____

_____

_____

_____

_____

_____

_____

_____

_____

_____

_____

_____

When have pharmaceutical medicine and intervention been valuable to you in your life? Where have natural alternatives been more helpful? What has deeply impacted your health and wellness in terms of approach? There is a place for both conventional medicine and natural alternatives; the skill is in reflecting on what is helpful in each context. If you know how to ask the right questions you can create effective and intelligent protocols and treatment plans. **What works for you?**

WOMEN'S HEALTH

Our hormones are tricky territory to navigate healthwise and I'm not convinced that shutting them down and replacing them with synthetics such as the contraceptive pill is the answer to problems in the wellness journey. Reflect on your journey with hormonal health. **What helps you to feel balance and wellness in this area?**

WELLNESS STRATEGY

When you are out of sorts do you have strategies in place to support wellness? Perhaps you have a favourite massage practitioner or acupuncturist you work with, or perhaps a long, warm, candle-lit bath does the trick? **How can you avoid sitting in a state of adrenal fatigue and stress and seek support when you're overloaded?**

_____

_____

_____

_____

_____

_____

_____

_____

_____

_____

_____

_____

_____

_____

_____

_____

_____

_____

_____

_____

_____

_____

_____

_____

_____

_____

SADHANA

Let's come back to the topic of daily conscious spiritual practice. **When do you make time for problem solving in your life? Are there small niggles you could fix that would give you greater mental clarity and space for joy? Who can you ask for help? How can you approach problem areas creatively?**

how well do you sleep?

So many people are struggling to get a good night's sleep and it's easy to get into bad habits. I've found the most important element to a good rest is in the preparation. Try to keep your mobile screen out of the bedroom and get off screens at least a couple of hours before going to sleep. Reading, meditating and yoga nidra (guided relaxation) are great alternative activities; gratitude practices and journalling are also beautiful bedtime rituals. **What does your perfect bedtime routine look like?**

BAD HABITS

Where do you need to implement boundaries in your life for better health and wellness: is it around screen time, or food? Who you are associating with? **Where do you need to clean up your act?**

Ever since I was a young girl I've loved making lotions and potions from plants I foraged. I grew up in the English countryside and enjoyed every minute I spent in the forests and woodlands of my childhood. We don't always need to reach for pharmaceuticals at the mere hint of a headache. Do you use herbs and essential oils as part of your wellness program? **How can you connect more deeply to Mother Nature's healing energy and support? How could you integrate more of nature's healing bounty into your life?**

CLEANING PRODUCTS

Take an inventory of your kitchen and bathroom cleaning products. How many chemical nasties are in there?

Can you declutter your products and make your own with natural ingredients or buy some eco alternatives?

'I BOW DOWN IN REVERENCE TO ALL MY TEACHERS'

Who are the people who have influenced your life for the better?

_____

_____

_____

_____

_____

_____

_____

_____

_____

_____

_____

_____

_____

_____

_____

_____

_____

_____

_____

_____

_____

_____

_____

_____

_____

_____

You can invite six guests to a dinner party, whether they are alive or no longer on the planet at this time. Choose wisely! **Who would you have at your dinner party to end all dinner parties and why?**

DO YOU LOVE SHOPPING?

Too often what we buy ends up in landfill, particularly when it comes to purchasing gifts. I invite you to pause and think about what you could offer as a gift that has a low impact on the environment. Here are some ideas:

- a home-made meal
- a home-baked cake
- some home-made beauty remedies and preparations
- a secret Santa offering rather than buying multiple gifts in larger families or communities
- an activity
- a charity donation

The possibilities are endless if you're creative.

Environment: make an offering. In the ancient Sanskrit scripture the Bhagavad Gita we are told it doesn't matter *what* you offer to God but rather *how* you offer. In other words, be humble and devoted to something higher than your own ego and make an offering of your life in service; in this way material items become less important. **What can you offer in devotion today?**

How can you be involved in supporting others to care more deeply for the environment, at work or at home? How can you be a better example?

_____

_____

_____

_____

_____

_____

_____

_____

_____

_____

_____

_____

_____

_____

_____

_____

_____

_____

_____

_____

_____

_____

_____

MOTHER
NATURE

HOW DO YOU PLAN YOUR MEALS?

Could you save time or money, or inspire better health through more mindfulness?

_____

_____

_____

_____

_____

_____

_____

_____

_____

_____

_____

_____

_____

_____

_____

_____

_____

_____

_____

_____

_____

_____

_____

_____

_____

_____

_____

_____

GO-TO HEALING MEALS

Make a list of your favourite healthy comfort foods and treats. **How does food nourish your soul?**

_____

_____

_____

_____

_____

_____

_____

_____

_____

_____

_____

_____

_____

_____

_____

_____

_____

_____

_____

_____

_____

_____

_____

_____

_____

_____

PERFECT BREAKFAST IN A GLASS

Smoothies are the summer go-to breakfast in my home. Ayurveda doesn't like too many crazy food combinations in one meal, so I try to keep things simple. My favourite ingredients are dates, plant-based mylks, frozen fruits and nut butters. Cinnamon or cardamom add sweetness without the need for sugar, and beetroot powder makes everything look pink so even suspicious children who are positioned against things that look too healthy get stuck in! **What's your favourite smoothie combo?**

Ancestral foods may not be the most healthy options available but they are filled with *prana* (life force) due to the place they have in your heart. For me, my grandmother's apple strudel is right up there at the top of the list. **What ancestral foods from your family or childhood do you remember with joy and delight?**

Prasadam is food that has been offered in gratitude before it's eaten. **How can you be grateful for the food you eat before each meal?**

hare krishna!

Hare is an address to God's energy, known as Radha, and *Krishna* is a name of God meaning 'He who is attractive to everyone'. *Rama* means 'One who gives pleasure and enjoys life'. The *maha* mantra is a prayer: 'O Krishna, O Rama, O energy of Krishna, please engage me in service.' The sound vibration of the mantra has a direct impact on the soul. Try it today; you don't need a special voice or special instructions. Chanting this mantra is the most powerful thing I do every day: 'Hare Krishna, Hare Krishna, Krishna, Krishna, Hare, Hare. Hare Rama, Hare Rama, Rama, Rama, Hare, Hare.'

LOOK AT THE FLOW OF YOUR DAY

Where do you lose energy and time to activities that aren't important to you? How can you better structure your daily routine to make it more joyful and aligned with your values?

WHEN TO DO YOUR SPIRITUAL PRACTICES

What times of day are most powerful for your sadhana?

The peacock feather is connected to Krishna and is a symbol of bhakti (loving devotion). Whenever I see peacock feathers I'm always reminded of the incredible beauty and mystery of Mother Nature; such perfection of form and delicate design can't be man-made. From the elegance of DNA structure to the peacock feather to our own bodies and their capacity to heal and transform, we are surrounded by magic and mystery in the most banal moments of everyday if we stop and look for it. **Where can you notice simple beauty in your daily life?**

ANCESTRAL TREASURES

Do you have any items of jewellery or clothing handed down from family that are precious to you? Do you feel the vibrations of elders when you wear these precious items?

How do you serve others in your life?

Where do you enjoy being of service?

Sometimes the simplest of gestures mean the most, such as making your companion a cup of tea or running your child a warm bath. **Can you anticipate a request from a loved one before they voice it?**

Could you repurpose and re-use something you already have rather than buying something new?

_____

_____

_____

_____

_____

_____

_____

_____

_____

Can you share the things of value in your life with others as a way of fostering community and connection?

_____

_____

_____

_____

_____

_____

_____

_____

_____

_____

_____

_____

_____

MAKING TIME FOR SOMEONE WHEN THEY NEED SUPPORT IS A POWERFUL GIFT

Can you give the gift of really listening deeply?

EMPATHY

Can you give the gift of empathy? **Can you put yourself in someone else's shoes when you are confronted by** them or in disagreement?

_____

_____

_____

_____

_____

_____

_____

_____

_____

_____

_____

_____

_____

_____

_____

_____

_____

_____

_____

_____

_____

_____

_____

_____

_____

_____

Do you spend a lot of time in nature? **Are there ways you could be more connected to the natural world?**

AYURVEDIC BEAUTY AND SELF-CARE

What could you do to simplify your beauty regimes? For example:

- switching to a wooden toothbrush (to reduce plastic waste)

- switching to a wooden hairbrush (recommended in the kundalini yoga movement to reduce static and care for long hair)

- aromatherapy oils (my favourite fragrances in the whole world!)

- neti pot and tongue scraping

KITCHEN

I love to make food staples from scratch that would cost a lot of money in the supermarket. It's usually better for your health, involves less packaging and costs significantly less. For example, I make a veggie stock that uses up veggies from the fridge that are past their best. The book *The Homemade Vegan Pantry* by Miyoko Schinner is filled with great ideas. Kombucha is another great option because it's easy to brew, is bursting with probiotics and costs next to nothing to make at home compared to the stuff you buy in the shops. **What food staples could you make from scratch?**

GIVING BACK

Reflect on the things you purchase regularly such as toilet paper or laundry powder. Many of these staples can be purchased from companies that give something back to communities in need or to charities. **How can you use the money you spend as a mindful tool for change? How can you vote with your dollar?**

SELF-CARE THAT DOESN'T COST THE EARTH

What could you do today that costs no money at all to love and nurture yourself, for example, visit the library, bask in the sunshine or cuddle your child?

INTENTION AND MANIFESTATION

THOUGHTS

Where do your thoughts hold you back? Do you get stuck in repeated stories or chatter in your mind? Do you shut down and get numb? **How would you like to transform your thinking?**

WORDS

When do you find yourself trapped in gossip?

_____

_____

_____

_____

_____

_____

When do you speak to your higher self?

_____

_____

_____

_____

_____

_____

_____

How can you spend more time speaking with words of sweetness and truth?

_____

_____

_____

_____

_____

_____

ACTIONS

When do you find yourself feeling you are in your most empowered state and strength?

_____

_____

_____

_____

_____

_____

_____

_____

_____

_____

_____

_____

_____

What activities light you up and leave you feeling full?

_____

_____

_____

_____

_____

_____

_____

_____

_____

_____

_____

_____

_____

_____

What are your biggest dreams and higher goals?

What do you really want that you are scared to name or say out loud?

RITUAL

Is there a place for ritual in your life? **Do you have a sacred space in your home that you could go to for grounding and solace?**

DON'T BE DISCOURAGED

Sometimes life is overwhelming and challenges feel too great. **What could you do to keep upbeat and encouraged during times of difficulty?**

LET GO OF RESULTS

The ancient sacred scripture the Bhagavad Gita emphasises that when we get attached to results we set ourselves up for disappointment and attempt to control situations we can't control. **Where can you let go and trust that the Divine Consciousness has your back?**

Sometimes from the sticky, icky binding of mud great beauty can emerge. Just as the caterpillar liquefies before it becomes a butterfly or the lotus flower blossoms from the muddiest waters below, you can emerge from your difficulties. **What are the biggest lessons you have learned from your darker times?**

Who inspires you because of the challenges they have overcome? What qualities does this person possess that you admire?

ULTIMATE MANIFESTATIONS

Have you heard the expression 'Be careful what you wish for'? **What are the highest dreams you are aspiring to in your life? Are they really what you want?**

let negative emotions move through you

Use your breath, particularly your out breath, to let go of that which is no longer serving you. **What do you want to let go of at this time?**

_____

_____

_____

_____

_____

_____

_____

_____

_____

_____

_____

_____

_____

_____

_____

_____

_____

_____

_____

_____

_____

Buddhist teacher Pema Chödrön is the author of a beautiful book called *When Things Fall Apart*. The book is full of gems of wisdom that create insight into our difficulties. **What have you learned in your life from times when things have fallen apart?**

Swaha is a Sanskrit word that means to let go and trust that Divine Grace has a plan for you. **Where in your life are you clinging on to a situation or person that is no longer serving you?**

What would letting go be like?

TRUSTED PRACTICES

It can be helpful in spiritual life to have certain practices that you return to time and time again. These practices become an anchor in our lives and see us through both ups and downs. Sometimes they are the practices you do even when you really don't feel like it, because you have a commitment to personal growth.

What are your trusted practices?

Wholesome ways to feel better: we all have unwholesome ways to feel better when we're stressed, anxious or overwhelmed. Some of mine include a glass of wine, vegging out in front of trashy TV and unconsciously bickering with loved ones. How could we redirect these choices to more wholesome ways of feeling better? For me, a long bath, listening to a spiritually uplifting podcast or cuddling with my kids work well. **Where do you make unwholesome choices under stress that could be redirected to something more nourishing?**

Author Biet Simkin writes in her brilliant book *Don't Just Sit There!* about the concept of 'pay for it first'. She states that when we really want something in life we often have to put in some hard work; for example, if you want a fit body you need to work out, or if you want to play the flute beautifully you have to practise. **Where in your life do you need to step up and pay in advance for what you want?**

Tapas is a Sanskrit word that means 'fire' or 'burning desire'. Tapas implies a commitment and sustained effort. It can manifest as a focus or fire in the belly that happens when you are aligned with your values and life mission. **Where is your tapas? What lights you up right now?**

Stories can be great for healing our hurts and confusions. For example, I love the mythological stories of Kali, a goddess warrior in her power and charge. **What myths and legends speak to you?**

_____

_____

_____

_____

_____

_____

_____

_____

What stories did you love as a child that have something of value in them for the now adult you?

_____

_____

_____

_____

_____

_____

_____

_____

_____

_____

_____

_____

Are you living in abundance and a place of financial empowerment, or do you and money have a difficult relationship?

_____

_____

_____

_____

_____

_____

_____

_____

_____

_____

_____

What are your strengths and weaknesses when it comes to your relationship with money?

_____

_____

_____

_____

_____

_____

_____

_____

_____

_____

_____

_____

_____

A *sankulpa* is a resolve or promise that you make to yourself, a mixture of setting an intention and holding an affirmation in your heart. **What is your sankulpa at this time in your life?**

WHAT ARE THE BIGGEST GIFTS YOU HAVE TO OFFER TO THE WORLD AT THIS TIME?

what are your blocks?

What holds you back?

_____

_____

_____

_____

_____

_____

_____

_____

_____

_____

_____

_____

_____

_____

_____

_____

_____

I was chatting with a friend about parenting. He had noticed that when he gave his children too many choices they got overwhelmed and couldn't make decisions. He thought that by giving them options he was honouring their sense of self and desire to self-direct, but what was happening in reality was the responsibility of too many possibilities was paralysing. To a certain extent in our modern world we all suffer a little from too many choices, and it can keep us from living in our true *dharma* (life calling). We all need boundaries; young children need more than adults to feel safe and held. **Is there a place in your life where you can impose some choice boundaries so you don't get paralysed into doing nothing due to being overwhelmed?**

Following on from creating choice boundaries: how can you focus on the bigger picture? When Barack Obama was president of the USA he famously often wore the same suit (in fact, he had several sets of the same suit in his wardrobe). When he was asked about this he explained that each of us has only a limited capacity for decision making in any one day. It's helpful to decide where we direct that capacity. In Obama's case he had world-changing decisions to make and didn't want to waste energy on deciding what to wear. **In your life, where do you waste energy on unimportant decision making? How could you redirect that energy to bigger things?**

WHAT DO YOU LOVE TO LEARN ABOUT?

Is there a particular area of learning that lights up your soul?

Could you find a mentor or take an online course on this subject?

PERSONAL GROWTH

What areas are you working on in your emotional life at the moment?

_____

Do you suffer with feelings of jealously or low self-esteem?

_____

How can you get support to grow up and out of these debilitating negative emotions?

_____

What do you celebrate in yourself in terms of self-development?

Where have you grown up the most?

What have you overcome with resilience that you are proud of?

In her excellent book *Big Magic*, author Elizabeth Gilbert reminds us that if we don't act on creative ideas when they come to us the energy may get lost and the idea may not even stick around! **What creative ambitions do you have that you've left on the back burner?**

INJECT SOME CREATIVITY INTO EVERY DAY

Where can you get more creative, for example, with your meals or clothing?

You might find it helps you to connect more deeply with loved ones who have different tastes to you if you cultivate an open 'give it a go' attitude. Do you always read the same types of books or watch the same types of movie? **How can you bust out of your comfort zone and mix things up a bit?**

not everything you do has to be amazing

Many of us get stuck in creative endeavours because we think if our artistic offerings aren't perfect they are worthless. Sometimes finished is better than perfect and an attempt is better than doing nothing. **What creative activities can you get started on today?**

fear can be our greatest teacher

What are you scared of?

_____
_____
_____
_____
_____
_____
_____
_____
_____

What does this fear have to teach you?

_____
_____
_____
_____
_____
_____
_____
_____
_____
_____

Our family ancestry, while often flawed, has so much beauty and healing within it when we remember the elements that uplift us. **What do you remember about your grandparents that is joyful and beautiful?**

DHARMA

What were you put on earth at this time to do? What are your deepest missions in life?

Where do you need more grace? Where would softening and letting go help?

How can you take one step towards light and joy today?

What tiny steps can you make now?

you've got to be in it to win it

Where are you holding back because of fear?

Ask for what you want. Do you feel like you deserve a pay rise at work? Do you wish your kids would put their dirty laundry in the basket? I do! From the trivial and mundane to the bigger picture elements of your life, asking for what you want often gets surprising results. **Where are you not asking for what you want?**

_____

_____

_____

_____

_____

_____

_____

_____

_____

How can you ask nicely and with skill?

_____

_____

_____

_____

_____

_____

_____

_____

_____

_____

_____

Better communication in intimate relationships: if you have a partner, spend some time journalling here about your style of communication. Have you got into bad habits of nagging or complaining? Are you kind and sweet? Do you look for the best? **How can you improve your communication with your loved one?**

How can you get closer to the Divine in your life? How do you connect to Universal Consciousness or God?

PRAYER

What are your deepest prayers and wishes?

What do you long for, for yourself and your loved ones?

What are your highest values and dreams?

SUBTLE
ENERGY

How do you protect your energy and vitality in difficult situations?

_____
_____
_____
_____
_____
_____
_____
_____
_____
_____
_____
_____

Where do you shut down, and how could you stay more open?

_____
_____
_____
_____
_____
_____
_____
_____
_____
_____
_____
_____
_____
_____

How does your energy interact with others?

_____

_____

_____

_____

_____

_____

_____

_____

_____

_____

_____

_____

What is the vibe of your aura or energy field?

_____

_____

_____

_____

_____

_____

_____

_____

_____

_____

_____

_____

_____

Before you interact with another person, how can you check in with yourself? Especially before difficult conversations or in confronting situations, how do you get grounded and steady?

TAKE A FEW DEEP BREATHS AND SCAN YOUR AWARENESS THROUGH YOUR BODY

Practise this energy awareness meditation whenever you feel overwhelmed or disconnected. Are there colours, sensations, blocks or areas that feel free and open? **What do you feel and sense?**

_____

_____

_____

_____

_____

_____

_____

_____

_____

_____

_____

_____

_____

_____

_____

_____

_____

_____

_____

_____

_____

_____

_____

_____

draw a picture of yourself

It can be abstract if, like me, you're not much of an artist! Inside the body of the picture write down all the words you would like to amplify in your life; for me some that spring to mind are 'love', 'patience' and 'compassion'. Draw a firm boundary around your body, a golden dome, and outside that dome write down all the words that do not serve you. 'Self-doubt', 'judgement' and 'neediness' would be some of mine.

FIRE ELEMENT

A burning desire for liberation is emphasised in Patañjali's Yoga Sutras. Fire has the quality of burning through impurities and resistance. In the sutras, the fire of tapas is connected to our capacity for discipline. In ayurveda the fire in the belly (*agni*) is responsible for digestion and assimilation, both of the food we eat and the things we need to digest in our lives, such as strong emotions or big life events. **How do you keep your spiritual fire burning?**

_____

_____

_____

_____

_____

_____

_____

_____

_____

_____

_____

_____

_____

_____

_____

_____

_____

_____

_____

_____

_____

_____

_____

_____

_____

SEX

How do you express passion and fire through your sexuality?

Is there a healthy place for this energy in your life?

ANGER

How do you express passion and fire through anger?

_____

_____

_____

_____

_____

_____

_____

_____

_____

_____

Is there a healthy place for this energy in your life, for example, as a spiritual activist?

_____

_____

_____

_____

_____

_____

_____

_____

_____

_____

_____

_____

_____

IMPATIENCE

How do you express passion and fire through impatience?

_____

_____

_____

_____

_____

_____

_____

_____

_____

_____

_____

Is there a healthy place for this energy in your life?

_____

_____

_____

_____

_____

_____

_____

_____

_____

_____

_____

_____

_____

ENTHUSIASM

How do you express passion and fire through your enthusiasm?

_____

_____

_____

_____

_____

_____

_____

_____

_____

_____

_____

Is there a healthy place for this energy in your life?

_____

_____

_____

_____

_____

_____

_____

_____

_____

_____

_____

_____

_____

The glue that holds things together: what do you get when you combine the two elements of water and earth? That's right: mud! Mud is sticky and dries out to become bonding, a glue of sorts. **Where do you need to find connections in your life?**

_____

_____

_____

_____

_____

_____

_____

_____

_____

_____

What would benefit from some grounding energy?

_____

_____

_____

_____

_____

_____

_____

_____

_____

_____

_____

_____

NATURE

How do you get grounded and steady through your relationship to the natural world?

_____

_____

_____

_____

_____

_____

_____

_____

_____

_____

_____

Is there a healthy place for this energy in your life?

_____

_____

_____

_____

_____

_____

_____

_____

_____

_____

_____

_____

_____

_____

_____

EARTH

How do you get grounded and steady through your relationship to the earth herself?

_____

_____

_____

_____

_____

_____

_____

_____

_____

_____

Is there a healthy place for this energy in your life?

_____

_____

_____

_____

_____

_____

_____

_____

_____

_____

_____

_____

_____

_____

STUBBORN PERSISTENCE

How do you get grounded and steady through your energy of stubborn persistence?

_____
_____
_____
_____
_____
_____
_____
_____
_____
_____
_____

Is there a healthy place for this energy in your life?

_____
_____
_____
_____
_____
_____
_____
_____
_____
_____
_____
_____
_____
_____

LOYALTY

How do you get grounded and steady through the expression of loyalty?

_____

_____

_____

_____

_____

_____

_____

_____

_____

_____

Is there a healthy place for this energy in your life?

_____

_____

_____

_____

_____

_____

_____

_____

_____

_____

_____

_____

creativity and spirituality often go hand in hand

What is your relationship with creativity like?

_____

_____

_____

_____

_____

_____

_____

_____

_____

_____

_____

When are you at your most spiritually connected?

_____

_____

_____

_____

_____

_____

_____

_____

_____

_____

_____

_____

_____

MULTITASKING

How do you get creative and spiritually connected through the expression of being able to hold space for lots of ideas and tasks at once?

_____

_____

_____

_____

_____

_____

_____

_____

_____

_____

_____

Is there a healthy place for this energy in your life?

_____

_____

_____

_____

_____

_____

_____

_____

_____

_____

_____

_____

_____

UNBOUND SPIRIT

How do you get creative and spiritually connected through the expression of your unbound spirit?

_____

_____

_____

_____

_____

_____

_____

_____

_____

_____

_____

_____

Is there a healthy place for this energy in your life?

_____

_____

_____

_____

_____

_____

_____

_____

_____

_____

_____

_____

_____

_____

BEING OVERWHELMED

How do you get creative and spiritually connected through being able to hold space for scattered mental states?

_____
_____
_____
_____
_____
_____
_____
_____
_____
_____
_____
_____

Is there a healthy place for this energy in your life?

_____
_____
_____
_____
_____
_____
_____
_____
_____
_____
_____
_____

COMMUNITY

How do you get creative and spiritually connected through making connections and bringing people together?

_____

_____

_____

_____

_____

_____

_____

_____

_____

_____

_____

Is there a healthy place for this energy in your life?

_____

_____

_____

_____

_____

_____

_____

_____

_____

_____

_____

_____

SPIRITUAL
ACTIVISM

Self-care is the act of creating a life you don't need to run away from. Rather than adding treats into your life in reaction to the parts you do under sufferance, the project becomes one of designing a life you want to live. **What changes could you make to create a life you love?**

the lotus flower blooms from the mud

Often (particularly on social media) what we see is the shiny, perfect-looking, beautiful version of people's lives, but without the water and earth combination of mud there can be no lotus flower. Most of the good things in life take a bit of work. A good relationship takes the investment of time and energy and a commitment to personal growth; a good career takes the investment of showing up and applying diligence and so it goes on. Make some notes focused on giving back and working through some mud, so the lotus of the heart can blossom. **How could you always leave a situation better than you found it?**

_____

_____

_____

_____

_____

_____

_____

_____

_____

_____

_____

_____

_____

_____

_____

_____

_____

_____

_____

_____

_____

_____

_____

TUNE IN TO THE ENERGY AROUND YOUR HEART SPACE

What do you feel there?

_____
_____
_____
_____
_____
_____
_____
_____
_____
_____
_____
_____

What words or images describe the vibration of your heart centre right now?

_____
_____
_____
_____
_____
_____
_____
_____
_____
_____
_____
_____
_____

beauty

What does it mean to be beautiful? I've noticed that true beauty has little to do with what a person looks like and everything to do with the grace with which a person holds themselves. People who live in service, who are kind and compassionate and genuinely interested in the well-being of others, radiate beauty. **In a world where people are spending more and more money on body modification, surgeries and expensive products in the name of beauty, how can you go back to basics?**

Making your own simple beauty preparations is a wonderful practice; you can do almost everything with coconut oil, for example! Used coffee grounds are another great item. This simple approach to daily grooming will save you money, save wasteful packaging that impacts the environment and leave you feeling radiantly beautiful from the inside out. **Where can you simplify your beauty regime?**

_____

_____

_____

_____

_____

_____

_____

_____

_____

_____

What products would you like to replace with something home-made?

_____

_____

_____

_____

_____

_____

_____

_____

_____

A PLANT-BASED DIET IS KINDER TO THE PLANET AND THE ANIMALS

What changes would you be willing to make to your diet and lifestyle in consideration of the environment and the other beings you share it with?

NATURE'S BOUNTY IS FULL OF HEALING PLANT-BASED FOODS!

These staples are so easy to add into your meals, drinks and smoothies and hold many health benefits:

- *Turmeric:* this root has so many powerful benefits, mostly in the anti-inflammatory department. Turmeric latte, anyone?

- *Ginger:* ginger is warming and nourishing, and is especially good for colds and sore throats.

- *Garlic:* this is a controversial one, as some practitioners state that garlic is stimulating for the mind and senses and might not help with your meditation practice. However, its immunity benefits are well documented.

- *Dates:* these are my go-to sugar replacement. I've started having a couple of dates after lunch in the afternoon slump instead of a coffee as a more sustainable pick me up.

What are you going to add into your diet to bring vitality and energy?

_____

_____

_____

_____

_____

_____

_____

What can you add, rather than focusing on what you might want to give up?

_____

_____

_____

_____

_____

_____

_____

What is your relationship with animals like? Do you see all beings as equal? How can you foster more connection?

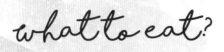
what to eat?

Look at how you could satisfy the part of you that craves snacks with healthier plant-based alternatives. For example, I can trade a cookie for a peanut butter, date, vanilla and banana smoothie — one of my favourite combos! — and still get a hit of sweet decadence. **Make a list of your favourite snacks and treats — not just the healthy ones, but all of them (for me it's cookies and sweets).**

where do you get stuck?

What are the triggers that have you falling off the wagon in terms of sticking to a diet that honours your highest values? Perhaps it's eating out or social family events. **Make a list of the places where you find it hard to eat well and then brainstorm some ways you could avoid this tension; for example, choose a vegan restaurant when you eat out or take something delicious that you've made along to the next family gathering.**

TRUST THE FOUNDATION OF HONESTY

Sometimes our loved ones tell us the truth and it hurts. **What home truths are you finding hard to hear at this time?**

_____

_____

_____

_____

_____

_____

_____

_____

_____

_____

_____

_____

_____

_____

_____

_____

_____

_____

_____

_____

_____

_____

_____

_____

If you are a parent, what mentors and teachers have helped you to cultivate the village it takes to raise a family? How could you upskill yourself as a parent?

SADHANA WITH CHILDREN

Are there children in your life who you would love to share some conscious spiritual practices with?

What might that involve?

_____

_____

_____

_____

_____

_____

_____

_____

_____

_____

_____

_____

Would your own inner child benefit from connecting to spirit at this time?

_____

_____

_____

_____

_____

_____

_____

_____

_____

_____

_____

_____

_____

_____

BHAKTI WITH CHILDREN

Are there children in your life who you would enjoy sharing some practices of unconditional support and kindness with? **What might that involve?**

_____

_____

_____

_____

_____

_____

_____

_____

_____

_____

Would your own inner child benefit from connecting to unconditional love at this time?

_____

_____

_____

_____

_____

_____

_____

_____

_____

_____

_____

_____

How can you be an example of non-violence and loving kindness to the children in your life and the children on the earth at this time?

_____

_____

_____

_____

_____

_____

_____

_____

_____

_____

_____

_____

_____

_____

_____

_____

_____

_____

_____

_____

_____

_____

_____

_____

_____

_____

Sometimes when we look at the world it all feels like doom and gloom, especially if you engage with the news. But humanity's evolution is not all bad news; while we still have a long way to go there are some incredible movements in the areas of gay rights, human rights, racial equality and women-focused initiatives. **What do you celebrate about the time and culture you are living in?**

How can you act now for future generations?

What calling (or dharma) do you hold in your heart that can serve a cause: animals, people, environment and so on?

WHERE ARE THE SMALL PLACES YOU CAN STEP UP FOR THE ENVIRONMENT?

I am committed to remembering my re-usable cup when I get a take-out coffee.

Hold space for your deepest healing: create a vision of the world you want to live in, a world young children can grow up in and thrive and flourish. **What are the values of this world?**

What are the priorities? Give this vision words and form.

GOODNESS

MERCY

GRACE

ARE YOU INTERESTED IN
LIVING THIS WAY?

LET'S UPLIFT EACH OTHER
AND KEEP UP TOGETHER.

HARE KRISHNA

A Rockpool book
PO Box 252,
Summer Hill,
NSW 2130,
Australia

rockpoolpublishing.co
Follow us! **f** 🅾 rockpoolpublishing
Tag your images with
#rockpoolpublishing

ISBN: 978-1-925924-47-3

Published in 2021 by Rockpool Publishing
Copyright text © Katie Rose 2021

Edited by Lisa Macken
Design by Sara Lindberg, Rockpool Publishing
Printed and bound in China
10 9 8 7 6 5 4 3 2 1